Lust at First Sight

By

Kizzy R. Wade

Copyright © Page

Ms. Kizzy Roshawnda Wade
Expressive Writings copyright@
3232 Bardaville Drive Apartment #2
Lansing, Michigan. 48906
Poetry Song Lust at First Sight

Acknowledgments

I would love to show gratitude to my High School Teacher, Ms. Joy, My Grandmother Princie Wade and John Wade. My mother Cathy Jones and Father Allen Jones, to my entire Spiritual Family. Brother Bobby Hemmitt, Antwain Jeffries, and my strong black sister who have been instrumental as effective motivators in my life.

I must appreciate my drive and ambition to produce all of my spiritual works of excellence. I have been writing poetry since elementary school. I have always been a creative and expressive young girl. I didn't like talking much shy as a mouse, but I thoroughly occupied myself with scholastic endeavors including poetry, writing stories, reading romance novels, and always imagining a world outside of my mind.

I will say thank you to my church family. I was enthralled in daily activities which triggered my creativity and spirituality at the same time. I would show my deep love and fondness for Reverend Shelton may he rest in peace. Mrs. Glover, Youth Director. I am so grateful for all of the time and discipline you instilled within me it really shape me into the woman I am I love you.

Gratitude is a display of appreciation shown with love, admiration, and fondness

About The Author

I tried to stand below the tree and feel the wind blow beneath summer's feet but I haven't quenched my thirstiness until I seen his perfect face. Come to me and do not delay. I have been dreaming and writing about you under this tree all day! Sweat drops run down my face profusely and as I lust for you my body began to ache. Why can't I touch him or say one word?

He got me hypnotized it isn't the sun's burning rays in my face. It's me imaging him holding me in a warm and intense embrace. I have been thinking about you since I discovered feelings of sexuality. My heart bursts with love, lust, and overwhelming bouts of fear.

Love, Lust was chasing after me and whispered in my ear, you can't escape my grasp I am right in front of you and this is when he appeared in front of me. O' help me my knees feel stuck in one place when can I move or am I forever in lust mistaking it for love?

Table of Contents

Introduction Page

Kizzy Roshawnda Wade

Falling *in lust is considerably similar to feeling the unexpected wisps of true love. Experiences of passion and a unique bond which is unmentionable places you in an entrance which is undetectable by the most frigid heart who resist the capture of love's snare but becomes aware of the insanity you are caught in.*

I tried to run away from the lust fullness but similarly love will grab you and pull into it's web of deceit tricking you into thinking you are definitely in love. I allowed my passion run a muck for twelve seasons of foolery. I unplugged my mind to reality and became irrationality in the flesh without flinching.

The most grandest time was hearing my soul sing and managing inexplicable happiness for a moment in time. I engaged in a risky, heart-breaking debacle filled with adventurous surprised and unending love-making which was very unimaginable to me but I desired to melt into my lover's arm's and feel him penetrate my entire mind, body, spirit, and soul.

Lust at First Sight

I can recall that cold winter night
that second it was Midnight.
I could feel your mesmerizing presence.
The fiery passionate yearning which ignited the moment I seen you look at me
so erotically my knees felt so weak,
my mind said don't fall to your knees yet.
Meet this man and find out what lustfulness lies deep inside his soul
because the day we both get in the bed and make hot sexy raw freaking sex
it's more than anyone could ever imagine and will ever know.
I felt a twinge from the universe and I said this is your Match-
You can lust for him and have unimaginable sex with him.
Your body will explode with heavenly orgasms,
filling up every inch of your body mind and soul.
I know I would be gratified in ways that nobody could even fathom and realized.
I felt pure love and lust at first sight.

Messed up over you

I am so messed up over you,
every thought I take I try to break up with you,
but my mind keep racing and anticipating what am I going to do
without hearing your sweet voice,
or feel your caressing touch, when you tell me you love me,
I know it's true- that every dam time I break up with you –
My heart shattered into trillions of pieces
and millions of my tears drops came running down my face
asking God what must I do so I could just see his face.
Those are the thoughts which run across my head if I left you
babbby,
I fight for the love I have for him and I ask myself?
Why do I love you Christian because you got me so messed up over
you?
My love keeps growing and passions continue growing deep inside
But I still haven't seen your face. Oh My God and this isn't no lie.
It's been nine months, long enough to give birth to our child.
And I lay her in my bed at night and try to figure out when will I be
able to look into your deep,
dark chestnut colored eyes
I will finally know why I am so messed up over you!

Broken-hearted

The first time I looked at you I knew you were going to be mine.

I began contemplating and reevaluating my thinking to myself and I said to myself,

Did I make a mistake about choosing you?

I am in utter turmoil agonizing about my crazy emotions for you but I don't know what to do?

You been putting me through so much shyt,

you been constantly running up my credit cards,

stealing out my purse, ferociously cashing and stealing my paychecks.

You left me broke and brokenhearted.

Why baby would you do this to me?

Loving you unconditionally.

You stole my heart right from the start.

The first glance it took at you. I gazed into o your dreamy endearing eyes.

I knew that my heart would be especially gone over you.
My mind, body, and soul was so eternally attached to you.
You used me up and I let you go.
Now I am free of you but I already know you are lost without me.
I am glad to know I made the best decision for me and it was to leave your ass behind.
It brought me the greatest peace and blessing to know we were done with one another.
I find so much comfort since I am starting over fresh without you in my life-and I am so happy I don't know what to do,
I have healed myself from the awful experience of being with you.
But you taught me perseverance and grace
so I didn't have much to lose only to gain.
I gained real knowledge and wisdom
something that I received from you so Thank you.
You gave me a gift you showed me exactly what to do
and that is not to share my life with you.
You didn't deserve me and you definitely left me brokenhearted over you.

How can I breathe or sleep?

I been standing here speculating out loud in my mind,
how did I allow you to walk all over my heart?
as I glanced at you laying here next to me.
I don't know if I should leave you or stay.
God please help me I am lost and confused.
I am puzzled swirling around in circles
trying to escape this labyrinth of my sexual inhibitions.
Is this labyrinth that I am trapped in love, a bond?
some deep powerful connection tells me
what is going on between us.
because I don't know I am going crazy over you!
Ooh Dear, I am not too fond of your manipulation and deception.
This is all too surreal;
My emotions are so wrapped up into you.
I began to suffocate
I can't breathe I must escape

run and hide from you so I can catch my breath so I can breathe.
I am loosing myself and this feeling is all too familiar.
I must acknowledge.
I need shelter from the pain I am experiencing with you.
How do I discharge your dysfunctional hold over me?
Will I stay forever in fear of losing you?
Myself?
What can I do with this love? hope for the best?
"I think not because my soul can't rest until I can breathe on my own again.

I Don't want to love again

My days seem so uncertain,
misplacing the love that I realized was never there.
It leaves me empty an unfulfilled,
how many men will I give my heart to?
and they throw it away in the garbage can,
I don't understand my heart is full of holes and darkness.
The brightness no longer exist;
Yeah they say the heart bleeds red blood-
but there is none that remain inside of these wretched heartless men.
These men drained my heart of compassionate love for them
and all I feel is rage and retribution-
this is the cost you pay when you allow men to play games with your heart.
Pretending to love you just get what they want from you.
Well I been going along with this illusion about love
and I have given up on love completely
I don't have no love left inside of me.
I don't want to love again.
No No No No love have left me alone so many times,
I can't count it's in comprehensible,
but I will say it one more time love just leave me alone.

Sex Fiend Lover

The first day I made love to you I felt that sexual spark that burst into flames
And I knew right in that second you were my sex machine.
Sex in the morning, Sex at noon time, and Sex at night.
I couldn't get enough of you- Even when I took a break from having sex with you-
You were all in my brain. Was the head of your penis or the first lick and taste of your skin which had me so sprung out over you.
I knew it would be endless night and days of burning, fanatical lovemaking.
This burning heaping flame could only be extinguished by you and no one else.
You are my sex machine I make love to you ceremonially in hundreds of positions.
And I make you feel so much ecstasy it is unreal.
I take you to so many dimension you haven't even felt before.
You can't ignore the chemistry and we share it is beyond approach and Oh so rare,
I won't stop being with you my sex machine lover.

Jailbird Lover

I rationalize thoughts in my mind the first time we spoke over the prison phone

that he would undeniably and could only be my jail bird lover.

I asked him when are we going to see each other and he replied.

Hold up girl, I'm locked up.

I still got some time to do- and I said how much time?

Sebastiano said you know I am doing a Bit-I said okay, silly me, I can't wait,

but in actuality the reality is that he turned out to be my jailbird lover.

Standing here in the cool midst of the night,

imaging him making steamy, sweaty love to me ever so intensely.

He stirred all of my senses, I felt him so suggestively, touching me, sensually as if he were in front of me.

I am holding him right invisibly experiencing the Oooohs, AAAhs

Although it was a figment of my imagination my mind indulged in a sexual fantasy.

Don't tell me this imposter pretending to love me and make empty promises,

Unfulfilling all of my request and leaving me disappointed

I digress for a moment let me take a minute to ponder and relieve my feelings of aggression.

I couldn't understand what was happening to me

But only I allowed him to dick fuck my brain while

I made myself go insane and I came so many times realizing what he had done to me.

And I must deny or at least clarify he had gotten too close to me.

Sebastiano must get a kick out of having a long distance woman-

I know he do because he laughs to himself constantly

saying she know that she got herself a Jailbird Lover!

Dope Fiend Husband

Every time you came home in a drug fiend frenzy,
Smelling like ten day old musty underarms.
I must declare it was quite sickening to smell his alcoholic breath,
And funky ass breath and please so ask me if he had the nerve to undress
And reveal his sexually stained underwear that was truly a nightmare.
It will make you feel very unimpressed. I don't care to discuss it,
But I must tell you about how it was to live with a dope fiend, alcoholic, cheating ass husband.
He's gone for days and weeks at a time driving around in my car in a dam daze.
Making up horrendous lies and I am clearly astounded and amazed by his deceptive nature,
I disengage and disconnect from his foolery
and tricks which were played on me.
I laughed out loud in disdain
over the ridiculous stories which come out of his disgusting mouth.

Waking up to a knock on the door 3:00 in the morning,
from his dope fiend girlfriend threatening to kick in my door
and beat both our asses shhhhyt,
But her real confession was girl I been fucking your dope fiend
husband.
Sorry to let you know all he cares about is snorting up so much
blow,
And spending your money on me and I love fucking your dope fiend
husband and it shows.
All I know is he had to go I packed my bags up quickly
And never looked back that right this is a true factual story of
living with my dope fiend alcoholic husband
and oh yeah that ho made sure she told me all about their nasty
sexual affair
but to her demise she was surprised that my husband wouldn't let
me go.
The woman became angry and went outside and keyed Bitch on the
passenger side of his car,
But she didn't touch my car it was a physical but subliminal
message
she had sent to my husband and it told him you better leave them
druggies alone.
But that's how it goes fucking with a dope fiend husband.

Death

Death is definitely associated with the living-
when our loved one passes on before us
we began to feel dismembered unattended and left alone
And feeling as if our life just passed us by as well
Why do we feel so lost and all alone?
When death and life arrive and leave without a moment's notice.
Wondering what's going on in the next stages of life seeking out
answers to our basic and sometimes
Irrevocably shaken emotions
Life's unexpected consequences
we face becoming accountable for our actions while you are
breathing
and interacting in God's miracoulouss place
Death is a transformation of life renewal of the soul
understand you must delete the old and welcome
the new splendid life waiting for you and it is eternally yours

Beauty

I have visualized colors, images, light, smiles, children's laughter,
and God's creatures running freely with no regard of any danger
or worry
and I imagine beauty's face Beauty is beyond our human's eye
sight
It is the what lies deep inside our third eye
in order to look at an object, place, human being animal or living
organism
you must possess beauty from within It began with you
and ends with you You should ask yourself how do I manifest my
own beauty?
Beauty is a rare gift given to some but not many,
We may judge beauty according to outward appearances
but in actuality most people don't know or realize how to acquire
Ms. Beauty
ask the Gods Goddesses heaven's above and below please bestow
beauty upon me
and I will forever be grateful and full of eternal happiness for the
most exquisite quality ever known to humanity

Encouragement

Kind words, spiritual affirmations, prayers, hopes, meditations
And goals are full of opportunities more than you can believe or perceive
How do I go forward with life aspirations and dreams?
listen to your grandmother, older sister, psychic medium, father, or pastor
realize these individuals were only spiritual stepping stones
towards you becoming this motivational visionary demonstrating
utter joy of pursing excellence very incredibly and systematically
reaping the benefits of hard work and sacrifice
this is what encouragement can bring

Follow Your Dreams

Eliminate failure form your vocabulary its non-existent to you
and me follow your dreams never give up get stuck or quit on what
determination and perseverance really means
believe in yourself acknowledge triumph, accomplishment, and
pure devotion to the task at hand
achieve what is true and destiny will follow greatness
You will pursue it in perfect orderliness
In order for you to create an awesome theme of excellence in your
life follow your dreams

Life

In a midst of a dream-fantasy I have experienced this lifetime before
I been here done that situation, circumstance
And I am telling you it all feels the same
I don't get mad at the outcome due to the fact there is no one to blame but me
I get frustrated at myself and say Kizzy You already know the future events taking place-
But at the same time I am enjoying life following my spiritual dreams
and this is a wonderful awesome future that I can certainly face;
In times of unpredictability only one can know indisputably
living every moment to its fullest is all that we can show
ourselves this is the everyday life I live life.

Loving me was it meant to be

I loved you for a lifetime
but you don't understand me
or acknowledge me for the woman I am
you sit there looking at me excitedly,
not knowing what to do with me.

www.ingramcontent.com/pod-product-compliance
Lightning Source LLC
LaVergne TN
LVHW041308150826
845673LV00008B/2802
9798664219241